WHAT EVERY AVERAGE GOLFER OUGHT TO KNOW

54 Easy Ways to Play Smarter and Lower Your Score

Presented by The Team at Golfwell

Published by: Pacific Trust Holdings NZ Ltd., 2017

This book contains Exercises and Drills. You should always seek medical advice from your medical professional and/or check with your physician before doing the exercises and drills in this book or in any exercise program to avoid possible injury.

PRAISES RECEIVED:

"A great book for average golfers to get rid and say goodbye to common mistakes which hurt scoring. It presents a smarter way to play – a true basic conservative game, and how to keep an emotional equilibrium when playing. Miracle shots happen more when you play smarter."

- J. Anderson, Rochester

"Good practical advice on common errors we overlook. Has drills and exercises you can fit into a busy schedule. A good reference book as a source showing it's not hard to play smart and conservative."

- E. Franks, Marco Island, FL

"A great read with accurate advice on avoiding needless strokes. Gives solutions and simple and easy ways to correct bad habits you normally don't think about. Golf is more fun when you use your head on the course. Great jokes too!"

- C. Trimmer, San Francisco

Contents

1
Par
4
•424 •398
373 •340

INTRODUCTION

Why is this book different?

This book is for average golfers *only* who want to easily score better and don't have the time to seriously practice because of other commitments with family and work schedules.

It gives you one source of 54 simple and easy things you can do that *will* lower your scores.

You will learn solutions to correct common golf mistakes.

You won't have to spend much time on the driving range banging away.

This book has simple drills and exercises you can do on your own when you have time. You will improve your scoring and enjoyment of the game.

You will establish good habits and play smarter.

SECTION ONE

STOP THE STRESS AND PLAY SMARTER: TIPS FOR THE DRIVING RANGE AND PRACTICE GREEN

1. STOP THE STRESS

If a golfer is in heavy traffic making him late for a tee time, stress causes the brain to release hormones in the body which are contrary to the relaxed tempo and timing necessary for a nice golf swing.

A Simple Solution: When you get to the golf course after rushing to make a tee time, practice slow breathing walking from the car to the pro shop to check in. If this isn't possible, do slow deep breathing when possible before teeing up.

Breathe in for 4 seconds and exhale for 6 seconds. Breathe slowly and fill up your lungs. The more oxygen your brain gets, the more you become relaxed. You'll swing better relaxed.

"Relax? How can anybody relax and play golf? You have to grip the club, don't you?"

-Ben Hogan

2. HOW TO FLEX AND LOOSEN UP.

Begin by stretching (squats, toe touches, rotating your upper body, etc).

It doesn't have to be elaborate stretching. Do your normal stretching exercises and repeat until you feel loose.

The Mayo Clinic has golf stretches to help you swing better and develop an excellent golf swing.

While you are doing these exercises, think about your short game. Tell yourself you are going to play an excellent short game today.

If you're going to hit balls on the range and are comfortable with your driving ability, warm up by making it "irons only". Irons will warm up your muscles faster. Warming up with irons only will make a difference playing the first six holes, rather than hitting driver at the range before playing.

3. KEEP YOUR CLUBS CLEAN.

Your golf clubs are your friends. Debris stuck in the grooves of your clubs will hinder back spin that automatically comes with hitting an iron with clean crisp grooves. Dirty clubs also make you look bad.

Washing your grips with dishwashing liquid will make the grips tacky so you won't have to add additional pressure to your grip.

Read up on your club manufacturers recommendations for properly maintaining them in a clean and excellent condition. Most golfers play better with regularly cleaned clubs.

Clean clubs mean less strokes.

4. REMEMBER AT LEAST HALF YOUR STROKES WILL BE CHIPS AND PUTTS.

EXERCISE: Go to the practice green, and begin by putting from off the fringe and watch the speed of the ball as it goes through the fringe. Watch the speed of others hitting putts too. Your brain will store this information. Hit putts just for speed.

Then practice putting using your pre-putt routine.

If you don't have a pre-putt routine, make one up for yourself since pre-putt routines are personal with each golfer.

Here's an example of a pre-putt routine:

1. Block all extraneous thoughts from your mind.

2 Do a 360 degree walk around the putting line.

3. Inspect the golf hole and observe the grain of the green.

4. Take a few practice strokes at the speed you want to hit it.

5. Take your stance and get comfortable.

6. Take two practice strokes.

7. Look at the hole.

8. Hit the putt.

Develop and do the same routine every time you putt. It will keep you in the present and clear your mind. You will save more strokes than you realize.

5. USE A HEAVY PUTTER ON FAST GREENS.

For the average golfer, a heavier putter will swing slower than a lighter putter. A short backswing with a heavier putter gives you less room to err than a long backswing and this is important for putting on fast and firm green.

There are also several putters on the market today with adjustable weights at your local golf store.

SECTION TWO

TIPS FOR THE FIRST TEE

6. TURN OFF YOUR MOBILE PHONE.

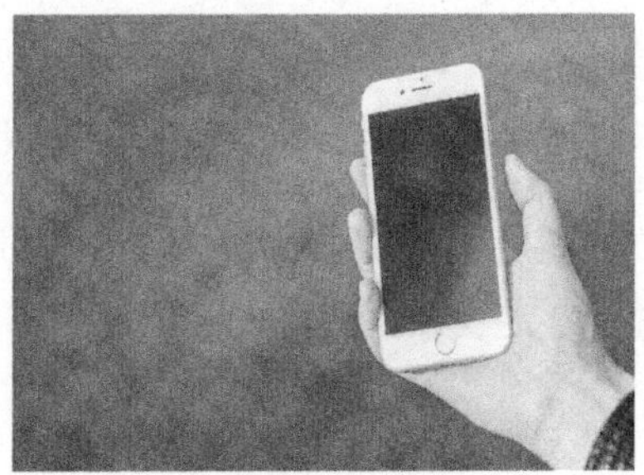

A very simple thing to do.

If you must stay in touch, adjust your cell phone setting accordingly so an incoming call won't bother another's game.

Some golf courses don't allow mobile phones on the course. If you don't take your phone, you can always call in when you have an opportunity like after the 9th hole or a delay in play on the course. Simply use common sense and be courteous.

"Technology is be our best friend, and technology is also the biggest spoiler of our lives."

"It interrupts our story, our individual thoughts, and our ability to imagine wonderful things as we become too busy from the cafeteria to the office on the cell phone."

-Steven Spielberg

As you may know, there are many golf GPS rangefinder apps in or for phones that give you shot distances, target and hazard distances, automatic golf course handicap calculator, etc.

Check the local rules of the course if you're not aware of their rules on mobile phones.

7. TEE UP AWAY FROM TROUBLE ON THE TEE BOX

Very simple technique. Simply tee up on the side of trouble to hit away from trouble.

This means teeing up your ball on the same side where there's trouble (trouble meaning: large trees, hazards, water, OB, etc. running down one side of the fairway).

If there's trouble on the left side, tee up on the left side of the tee box, so you're simply hitting away from hazards.

If your ball is teed up on the extreme left side of the tee markers, remember the rules allow you to take your stance outside of the tee markers.

If there's trouble on both sides of the fairway, you can tee up in the middle between the tee markers, or make an individual decision on which side has the most trouble, then tee up on the side to hit away from the most trouble.

Your chances of finding the fairway, and have your ball be hazard free when driving greatly improve when you tee the ball away from trouble.

*

A blonde, redhead and a brunette are teeing up on a mountain top tee box when lightnings blasts the three of them and in an instant all three are standing in front of the Gates of Heaven.

St. Peter is standing in front of the gates and says, "If you want to get through these Pearly Gates you have to pass the 100-joke test without laughing."

The redhead hears 37 jokes, but she can't hold back her laughter anymore and lets out a huge guffaw. St. Peter says, "Sorry, you've got to go to hell." Immediately, she drops down out of the clouds into a blazing inferno.

The brunette is next and gets all the way up to the 79th joke, and likewise busts out laughing and goes straight to hell.

The blonde listens intently keeping a straight face all the way up to the 99th joke, then busts out laughing. She's laughing so hard she's bent over gasping for air.

St. Peter stands there scratching his head and says, "The 99th joke is the worst joke of the bunch and you were so close to getting through these Gates, why did you laugh at it?"

Blonde says, "I just got the first joke!"

Remember to tee up away from trouble.

"Golf without bunkers and hazards, would be tame and monotonous."

"So, would life for that matter."

-B. C. Forbes

8. PLAY FROM TEES SUITED TO YOUR GAME.

Play from the set of tees that's right for you distance wise. It's more fun that way, especially since you won't be hitting a three metal all day on your second shot playing the par 4s.

One way to tell if you're playing the right set of tees is whether you can reach the green on two shots on the par 4s. If you can't, move up to the next set if it's not the lady's tees. If there aren't any other men's set of tees, do the best you can.

The long hitters in your group won't mind if you play from shorter tees. Your drive should be up to their drives. Another short hitting player in your group may even join you on the shorter tees. The game goes faster that way and is much more enjoyable. You'll be happier and play better.

Computerized scorecards normally auto adjust the handicaps based on the set of tees you're playing. If not, take a stroke from your handicap or whatever you agree amongst yourselves.

Senior golfers normally hit shorter than they used to. If you are a senior golfer, think positive about growing older. You should have less things on your mind when you're retired and enjoy the outdoors and fresh air and healthy exercise. Senior golfers tend to discuss and solve the world's problems on the course too keeping their minds active talking current events.

9. RELAX. DON'T PLAY THE GAME TOO SERIOUSLY.

When you're on the first tee, think about the others you're playing with. They normally don't want to play with a tensed up serious golfer.

Our definition of an "Overly Serious Golfer" is:

Overly Serious Golfer (OSG) is one who before beginning play from the first tee, self-appoints himself as "Golf Police" and inspects all golf bags, golf carts, undercarriages of golf carts (with mirror devices) to determine if each player is playing with 14 clubs or less. An OSG throws clubs, and shouts obscenities.

Most of us know mistakes will just happen in every single round, but mistakes happen less often if you are mindful of common mistakes set out in this book and how to easily correct them.

Even the great Greg Norman admits to making mistakes:

"Last week I made a couple of fundamental mistakes that I probably wouldn't have made in the heat of the battle back when I was in my heyday, but being aware of those things will make them happen less."

-Greg Norman

Over Serious Golfer

10. DON'T OVERTHINK THE SHOT YOUR GOING TO MAKE.

When you're on the first tee, or, before any shot to the green, there are only two questions to ask yourself:

1. Where do I want to hit it?

2. What club do I use to get there?

Simply keep your thoughts to these two simple questions before every shot you take from tee to green. This simple two thought approach to shots will make your game easier and lower your score. But, don't be seduced by the success you experience, as Bill Gates points out.

"Success is a bad teacher. It seduces bright people into thinking they can't lose."

- Bill Gates

11. USE DIFFERENT CLUBS OFF THE TEE.

Many average golfers want to automatically hit driver off the tee and it tends to automatically pop out of the bag by itself.

Once you decided the two questions of where you want to hit it, and how are you going to get there, consider using a club other than your driver.

Statistics show PGA Tour players who aren't exceptionally long hitters use their driver 72% of the time when playing a par 4 or par 5 hole.

The longer hitters on the Tour only use their driver 64% of the time on par 4 and par 5 holes.

The shorter hitters use their driver 81% of the time on par 4s and par 5s.

12. SWING EASY WHEN IT'S BREEZY.

"There's no place like home..."

Make sure you think about making good contact with the ball if you are hitting into a very strong wind. It doesn't matter what club you're using – driver or whatever – focus on making good contact.

Don't think about the wind when it's blowing hard straight in your face. After you've decided where you want to hit it, and what club to use, think about making a nice swing for good contact.

If you're wearing a hat, take it off so it doesn't distract you.

Hitting against the wind exaggerates draws and fades. So, take exaggerated draws and fades into consideration when you select the area you want to hit to.

Forget about putting any extra force in your swing.

Before you hit, keep a single swing thought in your mind like making a smooth swing, or good contact with the ball, or whatever gets your mind off trying to hit the ball harder.

If you're going to hit an iron into a strong wind, take the wind into consideration and add a club for each 12-15 mph of wind, or whatever you personally decide is necessary in accordance with the wind speed. If the wind is gusting, it's gusting for everyone and there's not much you can do - just leave it up to the wind gods.

You also increase the percentages of making good contact by using only three quarters of your normal swing speed.

To keep your ball low, play the ball farther back in your stance, and hit it with 75% power.

If you make a mistake going into a strong wind, remember what Dali said about mistakes.

"Mistakes are almost always of a sacred nature."

"Never try to correct them."

"On the contrary: rationalize them, understand them thoroughly."

"After that, it will be possible for you to sublimate them."

-Salvador Dali

13. TRY NOT TO STAND OVER THE BALL TOO LONG.

How long you stand over the ball before you hit it is an individual decision. Of course, if you stand over a ball too long, you may tighten up and increase the chance of hitting a bad shot.

Most PGA teaching pros agree on hitting the ball only a few seconds after taking your stance. Whatever time you take should be consistent with every shot.

After taking a stance over the ball, some players waggle to stay loose and relaxed like Jason Dufner, "I played a lot of baseball as I grew up, and I hit better if I kept moving before the pitch instead of standing still."

"A waggle does the same thing in the golf. It keeps you relaxed and gets you ready to hit the ball."

It's, of course, up to you whether waggling will keep you focused and relaxed. Since Jason Dufner does it, at least you know one of the best players feels waggling is part of his game, and essential to his play.

Your goal, like the goal of Jason Dufner is to stay focused and relaxed – simultaneously. The amount of time your stand over the ball is up to you and your individual style in setting up for a shot.

For some players, waggling relaxes your body, to allow your subconscious to guide you to hit the ball well.

SECTION THREE

EASY TIPS TO LOWER YOUR SCORE DURING THE ROUND

14. KEEP YOUR HEAD STILL AND BEHIND THE BALL.

Sounds simple, but this one thought is a big stroke saver.

If you don't keep your head motionless, you'll increase the chance of shanking the ball, or hitting it fat or thin.

Some golfers tense up and keep their head down and too still. They overdo it which results in a bad shot as well.

Keep your head still and behind the ball until the ball is gone and on its way to the target.

Don't reach down at the ball. Instead, stand tall in a normal stance like most low handicap golfers.

As you take the club away for practice swings, be aware of your left shoulder turning under your chin while you are keeping your left arm straight.

15. WHEN SWINGING, KEEP YOUR EYES ON THE BALL FOR TWO SECONDS.

Dr. Joan Vickers, Ph.D., a professor in neuro-motor psychology, did a research project studying how vision controls and modulates motor behavior with professional golfers and social golfers.

In other words, she studied a golfer's eye-tracking, and studied the differences between low handicappers and high handicappers.

She wanted to find out where low handicap golfers focused their eyes when hitting, and how much time elapsed from the taking the club back away from the ball to the finished swing where the golfer's eyes were taken off the ball.

She used headgear apparatus on the golfers which gave her information on exactly where the golfers focused their eyes before, during, and after hitting the ball, and for how long their eyes focused on the ball.

By comparing the results between high and low handicappers, she discovered most all golfers focus their eyes on the back of the ball, and not the top of the ball.

Physiologically speaking, the eyes give information to the brain, and the brain relays the information to the muscles telling the muscles what to do.

The low handicappers kept their eyes focus for 2 seconds while the high handicappers only focused 1.5 seconds on the back of the ball. The ½ second difference made a substantial difference in ball striking.

DRILL: At the range, hit a bucket of balls and focus your eyes on the back of the ball (rather than the top or center of the ball or the leading edge of the ball). Focus on this back of the ball spot before hitting the ball, keeping your eyes focused on this spot for at least two seconds from the time you take your club away.

Keep your eyes on the spot even though the ball has gone into flight. If you find counting to two is a distraction, simply tell yourself to keep your eyes focused on the ground behind the ball, and you will intentionally keep looking at this spot on the ground until after the ball is gone. This adjustment to keep looking down at the spot should add a half second as in the experiment results.

You should see a difference in your ball striking, and save strokes.

Focus your eyes on the back end of the ball

16. REMAIN CALM AND NUETRAL AFTER DOING WELL ON A GOLF HOLE.

*"After the Lord Mayor's parade comes the dust cart (or, the horse sh#*t cart)."*

- Anon

The average golfer isn't used to making birdies, or chipping in, or holing out from a bunker. A great shot changes your emotions, and hormones are release upsetting your normal balance.

Golf requires emotional consistency, i.e. a level temperament. Unexpected shots (like long hole outs, chip ins, very long putts) change your chemistry and affect your ability to play the next shot.

When good things happen during the round (say you parred the last five holes and your mind is reeling with excitement, "I'm finally going to break 90" and your body chemistry is changing your muscular system.

If you realistically want to reach your goal of breaking 90, get back to the present by doing deep slow breathing exercises for a minute or longer and relax. Have a clear peaceful picture in your head of a blue sky or whatever relaxes you, and you'll get back to normal.

If you can be consistent in your feelings, you will be consistent in your golf round and score better.

Golf scores going up and down have a direct correlation to your emotions going up and down. Practice deep breathing to get back to normal, and you'll save strokes.

"Consistency is contrary to nature, contrary to life."

"The only completely consistent people are dead."

-Aldous Huxley

17. THE GOLF BALL IS YOUR FRIEND, DON'T TRY TO KILL IT.

If you're in the middle of a round, and you find yourself (for some unknown reason) swinging way too fast, and slashing at the ball (this may happen if you unconsciously desire to force yourself to play better), understand the more relaxed you are, the better you will play.

Or, have you ever found yourself playing bad and no matter what you do you can't stop it?

Here's a simple 4 step solution to get you back playing your normal game:

1. Tell yourself you are going to just try to keep the ball in play. Take a deep breath, and pick a short area on the fairway you want to hit your next shot to. Focus on just getting it there and nothing else.

2. Don't take your full back swing. Take several slow three-quarter (3/4) practice back swings.

(Slashing at a ball starts when you have your club at the top of your back swing.)

3. Tell yourself you are going to rid yourself of the overkilling tendency.

4. Take the club back slowly. A quick takeaway leads to over swinging. Take a three-quarter swing and use only 70% of your power when bringing the club down and smoothly strike the ball.

Doing a three-quarter swing will work and save you strokes.

18. YOU DON'T HAVE TO HIT THE GREEN EVERYTIME.

Golf course designers usually lay out trouble around a green.

If you decide there's too many issues about going for the green (water, super deep bunkers, runoffs, etc.) it's usually best to layup.

It may not be as exciting as hitting a difficult green in regulation, but you will save strokes and feel much better after the round. There are no pictures on scorecards as they say.

So, select an area to lay up to and select a club to get you there safely. It's not complicated and you'll feel better and save strokes.

19. YOU DON'T HAVE TO USE AN 8.5 DEGREE DRIVER

You've heard the adage, "More loft, more control, period?"

Average golfers may think if they used the same equipment as the best players in the world, they will improve and save strokes.

More than often, you'll play worse. Some experts have the opinion the average golfer has difficulty hitting a TaylorMade M1 Driver which is used by a lot of PGA Tour players. The TaylorMade M2 is more forgiving.

On the PGA Tour, the average driver loft is about 9.5 degrees.

Sales statistics show the bestselling drivers that golfers generally buy at the retail counter are three kinds:

1. A 9-degree Driver

2. A 9.5-degree Driver; and

3. A 10-degree Driver.

The best players in golf want to drive the ball and keep it on the fairway. For the average golfer, the steeper the loft, the harder it is to control the ball off the tee.

The penalty for hitting Out of Bounds or losing a ball is stroke and distance. The average golfer will save strokes by avoiding low steep lofted macho drivers.

"Macho does not prove mucho."

-Zsa Zsa Gabor

EXERCISE:

If you have a 10 degree or less driver, play 5 rounds with a driver with a face having 10.5 degrees of loft, or more, (leave your steep faced driver at home, and use your three-metal instead of the driver). Keep track of your scores. Then play 5 rounds with your normal driver. See if you save strokes not using a steep faced driver.

20. ALLOW FOR ERRORS KEEPING AWAY FROM TROUBLE.

You are 165 yards away from the middle of this par 3 green. There's a steep drop off to the right of the green which goes down into a hollow (unseen in photo). There is a gradual slope off the green to the left.

If you go over the green, there is a steep drop off into the sea. The wind is blowing from left to right at 15 mph.

First decide where you want to hit it and what club you would use, knowing you don't always hit it perfectly. Think about hitting short to the left side of the green to prevent going over the green or down the right side steep slope.

Plan for every shot you take from tee to green on your next round.

"A goal without a plan is just a wish."

- Antoine de Saint-Exupéry

21. ERR TO THE SIDE OF THE GREEN AWAY FROM THE PIN.

You are 110 yards away approaching from the left side.

You feel you must hit it at the pin because you are losing your match. You want to knock it close.

There's room on the right side of the green - as you can see from the photo – leaving a fair amount of room for error. But it's a different story on the left side of the pin, and there's also trouble if you go through the green.

Conservative play would be to aim for the right side of the green, or aim for the middle. The percentages dictate you to do this.

If you don't like falling behind in a match, remember Jack Nicklaus kept a positive attitude when he was trailing.

"Being two strokes ahead going into the last day makes it easier to win, but it's probably easier to win coming from behind. There is no fear in chasing. There is fear in being chased."

-Jack Nicklaus

22. TRY NOT TO THINK YOU CAN HIT IT FARTHER.

Many times, we've read, "Play within your ability." But, you've made great shots in the past and great shots do happen. The average golfer may tend to think, "If I did it before, I can do it again."

But, becoming better at golf is a gradual process. If you don't play a lot of golf, play conservatively and you'll automatically score better.

Let miracle shots occur by themselves. You're more likely to experience miracle shots if you play conservatively.

"Play within your own game. Don't try to match your opponent's long drives or other shots. Play your own game."

-Bobby Jones

23. THE "UNPLAYABLE LIE RULE" IS YOUR FRIEND

Declaring your ball as unplayable is a way to save strokes rather than wasting strokes trying to chop a ball out of heavy rough.

The right to declare a ball unplayable applies everywhere on the course (even a sand trap), unless you hit the ball into a water hazard (where you have to drop it within 2 club lengths, no nearer the hole from the point the ball went into the hazard).

As to water hazards, make sure your ball is in the water hazard and not in "Casual Water" which allows a free drop no closer to the hole.

Once you declare your ball to be unplayable, you have 3 alternatives:

1. Go back to the point where you hit it from with one stroke penalty (i.e. you take a "stroke and

distance" penalty). If it was your tee shot, you go back to the tee and re-tee the ball and hit another ball, or

2. Take a drop inside two club lengths from your ball (no closer to the hole), or

3. Draw an imaginary line from the hole to the ball you are declaring unplayable and drop the ball anywhere behind your ball.

There's a one stroke penalty for all three options.

Players may be tempted to chop away, especially where the player doesn't have far to go to get the ball where it can be easily hit.

In the heavy grass pictured below, percentages dictate it's easier to take a one stroke penalty.

24. "HEY, YOU GROUNDED YOUR CLUB?"

You probably know you can't ground your club in a hazard area (e.g., water hazard, lateral hazard, bunker, etc.).

And, you probably know you can't remove loose impediments or touch the ground in any manner if your ball comes to rest in a hazard area.

An interesting example of not touching anything in a hazard rule occurred several years ago, when Michele Wie hit into a water hazard.

She was trying to make a par 5 on her second shot, but hit the ball into a greenside lake. She took her shoe off and put one foot in the lake and tried to hit the ball out of the lake. The ball only went about a foot in the air and came to rest *still* in the hazard.

Trying to balance herself after hitting the ball, she touched her club on the ground in the hazard area while her ball (which only went a foot in the air was still in the hazard).

She was penalized two shots which turned a par into a double bogey.

Her account of this was: "I knew that I did ground the club, that was a fact, but that was the only fact."

"I did call for a ruling; I knew I did that, but at the same time I knew that I felt off-balance."

"I closed my eyes when I hit the shot. I grounded my club to stop me from falling into the water and I was wearing a white skirt."

25. TRY IMPOSSIBLE SHOTS

"I always used 100% effort and I never quit trying. I never felt I didn't have a chance to win."

-Arnold Palmer

If you are playing a practice round and your score doesn't matter to you, it's fun to try an impossible shot now and see how you do.

Of course, regularly attempting low percentage shots isn't good.

If you have an impossible shot, be sure to consider all reasonable possibilities before taking an unplayable lie.

If there's a good chance of popping the ball out of the hazard or popping on to an area where you can get a good swing at it, then go for it.

Golfer's tend to gain more confidence by practicing shots they don't normally make. For example, hitting a ball partially or half submerged in a water hazard will make you learn the density of water, and what balls you can get out and what balls you can't get out.

"Nothing is impossible in this world if you put your mind to it and keep a positive attitude."

-Lou Holtz

26. LOOSING YOUR BALANCE OR YOUR COOL.

DRILL: An easy method of keeping your balance is to do practice swings before a shot with the sole purpose of having a good tempo and balance in your swing.

Go to the range, and do 25 easy practice swings just concentrating on balance. Then, hit balls with 75% of your power concentrating on keeping your balance.

If you watch Sergio Garcia do practice swings before he hits a shot, he does them solely to test and train his sense of balance during his swing.

Loosing balance usually comes from over swinging, or attempting to hit the ball further than you can.

Keeping a calm mind helps tempo and balance. Getting extremely upset over a bad shot may continue to bother you, and is something to avoid.

Ways to avoid getting overly upset after making a bad shot:

1. Ask yourself, "What is the worst thing that can happen now after that terrible shot?"

Make yourself aware of the "terrible things" that will happen to you now that you made the "devastating" shot, and you'll find it's really no problem.

2. Think realistically about your golf ability. Don't put pressure on yourself by demanding too much of yourself.

3. Understand bad or embarrassing shots happen regularly in golf to everyone, usually at the worst time, and when you least expect it.

*

Here's a story about keeping a cool head:

Tiger Woods decided to get married to a wonderful woman and they were deeply in love. He proposed and she accepted and they planned a large beautiful wedding.

At an extravagant wedding ceremony in a huge Church, the soft-spoken minister began the marriage ceremony. The Church became silent. The minister routinely asked if anyone in the temple had anything to say or a reason why the two should not get married, "Speak now, or forever hold your peace," the minister said.

There was a quick moment of utter silence which was broken like the blade of a pitching wedge striking a rock, when a beautiful young woman carrying a newborn baby stood up in the last pew, and started walking toward the minister slowly.

The newborn's cries and whimpers echoed as the young girl continued to approach the front of the church.

Chaos ensued quickly. The bride slapped Tiger. The groomsmen winked at each other, and the wide-eyed bridesmaids couldn't believe what they were witnessing.

The bride's father got up and took a wild swing at Tiger, then put his arm around his daughter, and took her out of the church.

Tiger couldn't believe what was happening, but stood his ground as the young woman and newborn approached him and the minister.

Most of the wedding guests got up and began to head for the exits.

The minister asked the woman, "Can you tell us why you came forward? What do you want to say?"

The young woman replied, "We can't hear in the back."

"Keep cool; anger is not an argument."

- Daniel Webster

27. TAKE A FULL SHOULDER TURN.

A full shoulder turn is essential in your swing. Don't shortcut the turn by overusing your arms.

Turn your left shoulder all the way so it turns under your chin (as you can see in the picture that follows).

If you find yourself hitting erratic shots, a lot of the time it's due to not turning. You may be picking the club up with your arms instead of turning your shoulders to begin your takeaway.

When you turn your shoulders, you are adding a lot of torque and power to hitting the ball further with less effort.

Are you making a good shoulder turn?

28. DON'T DWELL ON THE PAST.

Common courtesy and consideration for others should stop you from saying things like:

1. "I should have used my (whatever) iron" (No one cares).

2. "This wind is always against me on every hole."

3. "Why did my ball roll off the green?"

Complaining makes golf worse.

"Most people won't want to spend time with you if you are someone who is most of the time angry or complaining."

- Stephen Hawking

29. HAVE A POST-SHOT ROUTINE.

Have a "Post-Shot Routine" to use when you need it after an embarrassing shot or bad hole. A good post-shot routine will help you play better, and not three or four putt the next green (saving strokes).

An example of a post-shot routine:

1. Allow yourself to fume for up to 15 seconds or less. Let it all out within reason.

2. After 15 seconds, do deep breathing until your head begins to clear.

3. Force a smile.

4. Think about your next shot to get back to the present.

30. TAKE AIM AT A SMALL TARGET.

"Q. What did I tell you about shooting?"

"A. Aim small, miss small."

-The Patriot

Average players sometimes think of just hitting the ball "somewhere" onto a wide-open fairway. It's better to first select a general area as your target.

After picking a general area you want to hit to, and after deciding on a club that will get you there, select a smaller target in that area.

On any shot (or on long putts), you can also pick out a small target behind the area you want to hit to (or putt to), like a large tower beyond the fairway (or a 3 foot in diameter circle around the hole).

Good golfers pick small targets and line up to small targets. Study the picture below:

You are on the 165-yard par 3 again. The pin is back on the right side. But, there is a steep drop off on the right side you can't see in this picture, and you don't want to hit it to the right.

The wind is blowing left to right at a medium speed. You could draw it to the middle of the green, But the middle of the green isn't a small target. You decide to aim at a small target which is the far-right side of the Ailsa Craig Rock where the right side of this Rock meets the sea.

31. DON'T TRY TO HELP THE BALL INTO THE AIR WHEN HITTING TO AN ELEVATED GREEN.

If you're more than 100 yards away from the pin, and hitting to an elevated green, a golfer may subconsciously try to scoop, or help lift the ball into the air.

To keep it simple, hit a normal shot but consider adding a club and hitting it high (i.e. play the ball a bit more forward).

"Life is simple, but we insist on making it complicated."

- Confucius

32. TREES AREN'T REALLY 90% AIR.

If you hit into a stand of trees and you find you're surrounded by large tree trunks, it's smart to play the percentages even if you must hit the ball backwards to get it back to the fairway.

Most average golfers have been in the situation where there is a gap to hit the ball through, and you may have been successful in the past shooting through narrow gaps. To save strokes, be conservative, and chip out as safely as you can.

33. DON'T BE OVERLY CONCERNED ABOUT YOUR SCORE.

Eighteen holes usually takes 4 hours to play. If things aren't going well, and you don't know why, the last thing to do is to get down on yourself. Understand bad shots are part of the game.

Even today's best players, and the best players who have ever played the game like Hogan, Palmer, and Nicklaus, were at no time perfect at it.

Knowing mistakes happen in golf, makes you calm and relaxed.

Take deep breaths to get more oxygen to your brain and help you relax. Once you're relaxed, calmly think about fixing your game and ask yourself questions:

1. Am I rushing my swing?

2. Keeping my head still and behind the ball?

3. Swaying instead of turning?

Or ask someone what they think might be the problem, but only if you're playing social golf and not in a competition. The rules don't allow you to ask or give advice on what may be wrong with your manner of play.

Step back if you feel tense before hitting any shot (or putt). When you're calmed down and relaxed, think positive about hitting a normal shot and tell yourself you're going to do that. Take deep breathes to get more oxygen. Do a pre-shot routine and swing smoothly. Think positive, avoid worrying.

"Worrying is like praying for something you don't want to happen."

-Robert Downey, Jr.

34. USE YOUR HYBRIDS MORE.

Long irons are difficult clubs to use for average golfers. If you still have a 3, 4 or 5 irons, replace them with comparable hybrids.

Hybrids have the bottom edge of the face of the club slightly forward of the hosel and shaft. This design made the hybrid popular as an easier club to hit. It can be used almost anywhere from tee to green.

If your ball is on the collar, or fringe of the green and against long grass, use the hybrid as you would a putter. Practice this shot to get a feel for distance when you use it like a putter.

Padraig Harrington used a hybrid to tee off on the last three holes in his British Open playoff victory against Sergio Garcia at Carnoustie. He considered the hybrid as his most reliable "Go To" Club.

35. DON'T HIT SHOTS YOU REALLY DON'T WANT TO.

Assume you've hit your ball into the middle of the bunker pictured above. The rest of your group are on the green. They've already marked their balls.

You want to hit a high shot out of the bunker and plop it on the green and have it roll close to the pin.

You've made this bunker shot before, but left it in the bunker half of the time.

You can bail out to the right and then pitch it on the green. But you dismiss that thought.

You are ready to hit. You look up at the flag and you notice the other 3 players are shifting their weight back and forth impatiently waiting for you.

The easy shot is to hit it out to the right. But you decide to go for the pin and plop it on the green. You rush your shot and leave it in the bunker.

You've become slightly angry. You slash at it again and watch the ball go almost straight up in the air, then plop back down into the bunker.

You know you should have hit it out to the right, then pitch it on or even roll it on the green using an iron or a "Texas wedge," or whatever club you feel comfortable with to get it close to the hole.

You'll save strokes by playing the higher percentage shots.

EXERCISE:

Make a small percentage symbol like this and tape it on your golf bag where you can easily see it when you take out a club as a reminder to play higher percentage shots:

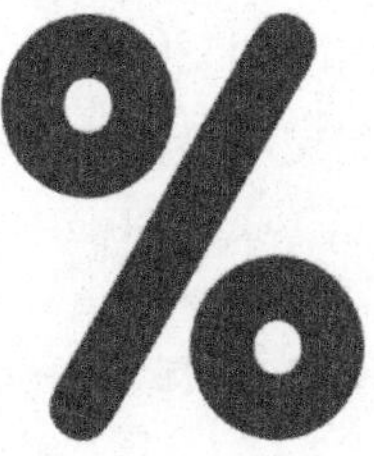

"The difference between stupidity and genius? Genious has its limits."

-Albert Einstein

36. DEAL WITH WHAT'S HAPPENING NOW.

Emotions arise from thinking about past events, or thinking about the future. If there is an annoyance while you are focusing, pause, and take a deep breath before you hit your shot.

"Mindfulness Meditation" is nonjudgmental meditation of the present. It helps you to clear your mind and block negative past events, and future events from entering your mind by thinking about the task at hand. See this YouTube for an example of Mindfulness Meditation which should help your golf game.

Being nonjudgmental will save you strokes.

37. NEVER GIVE UP!

Ernie Els, a winner of four-major titles, six-putted for a quintuple bogey (a score of 9) on the first hole in the first round of 2016 Masters Tournament.

The quintuple bogey set a record as the highest score ever recorded on the first hole in the Masters.

In contrast, Ernie's opening round the year before was a 5 under 67.

He didn't give up, and finished the opening day with a round of 80.

On the second day, he made a few birdies and sank some great putts shooting one over for a 73.

He commented after his second round, "I was almost getting back to normal."

Some of greatest players in the world have bad days. Ernie didn't give up after shooting a 9 on the first hole.

If it can happen to Ernie Els, it can happen to anyone. Crazy things happen in golf, and will continue to happen during your golfing days so take the bad and the good and keep positive.

"Our weakness is giving up. The most certain way to succeed is to try just one more time."

-Thomas A. Edison

*

Ernie Els died and was up before God for Judgment. He was met by St. Peter at the Gates of Heaven who greeted him. "Mr. Els, you were a great golfer but before you meet God, I thought I should tell you that other than your great golf career, you really didn't do anything for the common good, or for the bad, so we don't really know what to do with you?

We don't have any golf courses in heaven but what particularly did you do on earth that was good?

Ernie pondered for a bit and said, "Once after playing a golf tournament in California, I was driving back to the hotel and there in the parking lot, I saw a young woman being tormented by a group of Hell's Angels – you know revving their engines, circling her, taunting her with obscenities?"

"Go on," said St. Peter.

"So, I stopped and got out of my car with my 5-iron and went up to the leader – the biggest guy there. He was much bigger than I, very muscular, had tattoos all over, a scar on his face and a ring in his nose. Well, I put my index finger in his nose ring and tore it out of his nose. Then I told him and the rest of them they'd better stop bothering this woman or they all would get more of the same!"

"Wow, that's very impressive Ernie!" St Peter replied. "When did this happen?"

"About two minutes ago," said Ernie.

38. AVOID STANDING TOO CLOSE OR TOO FAR AWAY FROM THE BALL.

Standing too far from the ball easily results in mishits. Standing too close causes problems too.

The proper distance you should be away from the ball is to take your normal golf stance - like a football linebacker stance with your back slightly leaning forward and knees slightly bent. Let your arms hang straight down (allow gravity to pull them straight down).

Grip the club and the point where the bottom of the club rests on the ground, is the correct distance you should be away from the ball.

To double check your distance to the ball, take your stance with your knees slightly bent and lower the end of the handle of your club to your upper right thigh. The end of the handle should touch about a half inch to an inch above the top of your kneecap.

39. YOU CAN HANDLE GREENSIDE BUNKERS.

Do you have trouble with greenside sand bunkers?

Think of sand shots as a "sand" shot. That is, you are not hitting the golf ball at all. You are having the leading edge of the bottom of your sand wedge enter the sand behind the ball, and lifting sand out carrying the ball with the sand.

For example, if there was a pebble in the sand instead of the ball, hit the sand behind the pebble to lift the pebble out.

There's a tendency to aim at the back of the golf ball, and you wind up hitting the ball instead of the sand.

The sand you splash out with your club will carry the pebble (i.e. the ball with it).

Aim so you club enters the sand an inch behind the ball and follow through.

DRILL: Practice bunker shots. Start with 15-minute sessions devoted only to sand shots. Notice how far the ball travels depending on how much sand you take each time.

Sand shots: Strike the sand behind the ball and let the sand carry the ball out of the bunker.

You'll save strokes and feel more confident on your approach shots to the green.

40. DO YOU HAVE THE RIGHT FLEX IN YOUR CLUB SHAFTS?

Golf shops and golf professionals have golf ball radar tracking devices to determine your swing speed, ball flight, ball spin, etc.

Schedule an appointment to have your swing and clubs looked at by a golf professional. The professional may give you clubs with different shafts to see what's best for you.

See the following chart on club shafts based on your swing speed.

Radar devices are very useful to get the right facts when you swing a club hitting the ball. Check with your golf shop or club professional to get their advice and have them put your swing on radar.

DRIVER

Swing Speed

Tempo	<70	70-80	80-90	90-100	100+
Fast	S	R	SS	XS	XS
Moderate	L	S	R	SS	XS
Slow	L	S	R	SS	SS

Ladies = L

Seniors = S

Regular = R

Stiff Shaft = SS

Extra Stiff = XS

41. DON'T MAKE EXCUSES OR BLAME OTHERS.

You look weak when you make excuses for a bad shot. Others think you're asking them to sympathize with you.

On the lighter side, make a fun remark after a bad shot (depending, of course, on who you are playing with):

1. "I shouldn't have drunk that Fifth of Jack this morning."

2. "I'm not used to playing with normal people like you guys."

3. "You shouldn't have told me we ran out of beer."

Or whatever.... Keeping it fun will help you relax, and save strokes.

42. BE SOCIABLE.

If you're playing in a big money, or big prize golf tournament, it's can be serious stuff, of course. You're not there to socialize. You're there to win.

But when playing serious golf, you may be adding unnecessary pressure to your game.

Socialize, and be friendly and complimentary but try not to talk about yourself. Ask them what's happening in their lives. Being with friends and playing golf is great for the spirit and you'll save strokes and play better.

43. THERE'S MANY WAYS TO PLAY A GOLF SHOT.

It's good to have a creative mind during a round of golf. You can pitch and run balls up on to the green with a seven iron or fly it to the green with a wedge. You can use a three-wood to putt a ball that came to rest against the collar of the green, etc.

There's a large variety of different golf shots: chop shots, flop shots, pitch shots, chip shots, lots of different approach shots, knock down shots, run ups, etc. giving you various ways to get the ball to your target.

You'll save shots by being creative with shots.

EXERCISE: Take a brief time-out, and think of different ways to play the shot. It sounds basic, and average golfers (at times) don't bother about being creative.

Being creative will save shots. If you get bad feelings about the shot you are about to play, pause and think of other ways to get the ball to your target.

As a change of pace, if you play regularly with the same group, suggest a two club or a three-club only competition for one round. All players can only use two or three clubs of their choice to use during a golf round. You will learn new shots which you may use in future rounds.

44. ROUTINES.

Another sample pre-shot routine is the Five-Step VAGSE Method:

Visualize

Align

Grip

Stance

Easy

Step 1. Visualize the shot. On the practice tee and the chipping green, visualize each shot before hitting it. Continue visualizing each shot from Tee to Green.

Step 2. Align the shot before you take your stance. Pick a spot on the ground (an odd blade of grass or dirt) just about a yard in front of your ball on the line to your target.

Step 3. Grip:

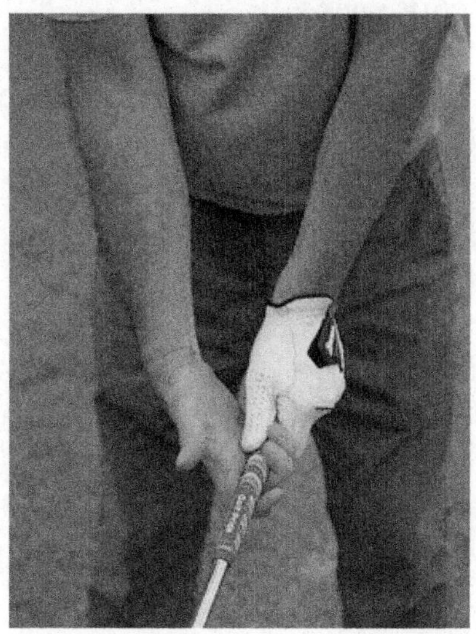

Use your normal grip with a light pressure (a 4 or 5 on a scale from 1-10).

Step 4. Stance. Take your stance and grip the ground with your feet. Check your ball position for the type of shot you want to hit.

Let your subconscious take over. If you feel comfortable, your stance should be fine. If not take a step back and let your thoughts clear.

Step 5. Swing Easy or in other words "Swing smoothly". Don't kill the ball and let the club do the work. Trust your swing.

For putting, develop your own pre-putt routine. Here is a simple pre-putt routine:

1. Walk 360 degrees around your putting line to view the entire putt from all angles.

2. Stand behind the ball and walk half way down the line and view the putt again.

3. Return to standing behind the ball and practice the tempo you are going to use to make the putt.

4. Take your putting stance and get comfortable and adjust your footing.

5. Take one more look at the hole, then hit the putt.

Doing the same routine from tee to green will save shots.

SECTION FOUR:

IN AND AROUND THE GREEN

45. CHIP RATHER THAN PITCH.

Around the green, average golfers tend to hit a pitch with a lob wedge high in the air letting the ball fall a few yards in front of the hole, and roll the rest of the way to the hole.

A chip may be better if the ball is about 10 feet away from the edge of the green. A chip allows the ball to roll on a low trajectory and run up to the hole.

Generally, a chip is more reliable to keep the ball in the right direction toward the hole. Pitching with a lob wedge may result in the club getting caught up in the grass, when trying to pitch the ball high into the air.

A chip pops the ball off the clubface (like you're chipping wood) on a low trajectory having the ball go only about 25% of the distance in the air and rolling the rest of the distance to the pin on the green.

"As a kid in Fayetteville, N.C., I spent hundreds of hours around the greens on the course my dad owned, hitting every shot I could think of - the one-hop-and-release, the chip that lands dead, the explosion from a bad lie."

-Raymond Floyd

46. USE YOUR PUTTER INSTEAD OF CHIPPING.

If your ball is on the fringe just off the green, most players will chip it on to the green using various irons from a 5 iron for longer chips and higher numbered irons up for shorter chips.

If your ball comes to rest near the green on hard pan, you might chunk a chip using an iron. You will save strokes by using your putter if you are less than 20 feet off the green putting over hard pan or firm ground.

Remember to judge the speed putting through longer grass.

47. OBSERVE THE CONTOUR OF THE GREEN AS YOU WALK UP.

Some average golfers with excellent feel, believe two putting isn't that hard and tend to get bored.

Putting is can be almost 50% of the strokes in a round. Taking putting seriously can dramatically lower your score.

Most average players usually start reading the green when they're on the green standing behind their ball getting ready to putt it.

Begin looking at the contour of the green as you are walking up to the green. Feed your brain with information on the general slope and surrounding areas. A green which appears to be flat, may not be flat at all when compared with the surroundings.

Three putts (or more) happen when the first putting attempt is a bad one leaving a long second putt.

After you take in the contour, use your pre-putt routine, and take your time. It will save strokes.

48. OVERREADING SHORT PUTTS.

"A three-foot putt is more nerve-racking than a nine-foot putt. You're expected to make the three-foot putt. There's always a chance a nine-foot putt, won't go in."

-Lydia Ko

You can overread any putt and become obsessed with it. You may wind up hitting short putts with more speed to take the break out – hitting it way past the hole if you miss it.

On long double breaking putts, some golfers think the ball will break less on the first break since the ball will be going faster through the first break.

Although this is partly true if you hit the putt firmly, on fast greens you should allow for both breaks or you will be under reading the putt.

Tiger Woods said, "The best way to handle pressure is a pre-putt routine."

Tiger added, "Don't deviate from your routine. A routine frees your mind, so you can deal with the task at hand."

"Pressure is something you feel when you don't know what the hell you're doing."

-Peyton Manning

49. SHORT BIG BREAKING PUTTS.

The most difficult putts are ones that break more when hit with less speed. For example, a five-foot putt with a large amount of break is a very difficult putt since it will break differently based on speed.

The easiest way to handle these five-foot putts (or any short heavy breaking putt under 10 feet) is to follow these two steps:

First Step: Decide the distance speed. Determining the right speed will at least leave you very close to the hole (and avoid going a long way past the hole and end up three-putting). Look at the speed factors such as the grain, uphill or downhill, etc.

Second Step: Once you determined the speed, you study the break. Decide on a break and go for it. If you don't decide, you will most likely hit a bad putt based on your indecision. The important thing is to decide on how much you believe the putt will break and hit it at the right speed and line you decided upon, and *stick* with it - without hesitating.

50. GETTING YOUR PUTT TO THE HOLE.

Leaving a putt way short can be annoying. Here's a drill that will correct it and get your putt to the hole and in range to easily make the second putt.

DRILL: Stand 7 feet from the hole and use 5 balls. Place a marker about 20-24 inches behind the hole. Putt all five balls until you have putted all the 5 balls either in the hole, or stopping past the hole but before the marker 20-24 inches behind it.

Once you have done this with 5 balls, back up to 14 feet from the hole and do the same drill putting the balls either in the hole, or past the hole stopping before the marker behind it.

Work up to 21 feet from the hole, and if you like, keep moving back to where you cannot get all 5 balls in the hole or not past the marker behind it.

SECTION FIVE:

AFTER THE ROUND

51. SOME GOLFERS DISSAPEAR INTO THE TOILET WITH A MAGAZINE FOR A HALF HOUR TO GET OUT OF PAYING FOR DRINKS WHEN YOU LOSE A MATCH.

Vince Lombardi said, "Winning isn't everything, but wanting to win is."

Joe Namath said, "You learn how to be a gracious winner and an outstanding loser." It goes without saying, it's always best to be a good sport whether you want to be a good sport or not.

You'll save strokes by treating those "two imposters winning and losing the same." You'll have peace of mind - whether you're up or down in a match.

52. REVIEW THE SCORECARD AFTER A ROUND TO SEE WHERE YOU NEED PRACTICE.

As you look at your score card and reflect on your round, think about areas you need to practice.

More likely than not, most wasted strokes will be in the short game area. Practice where you're weakest when you have time. You'll save more strokes the next time you play.

53. SAVE STROKES WITH NEW GRIPS.

Talk to your golf professional about whether you need new grips, and the type of grips that suit your game. Making an adjustment to use good grips will save strokes.

Washing your grips in dishwashing liquid will make them tacky and easier to grip.

Seniors: Talk to your golf professional to see if arthritic grips will help your game.

54. KEEP CURRENT ON GOLF NEWS.

New golf ideas are occurring all the time. Learn more about the golf world and your game.

Read how you can improve your game in Golf Magazines, Golf Websites, such as Golf.com, GolfDigest.com, GolfChannel.com, PGATour.com MyGolfSpy.com and many, many more.

There are a lot places to go and a lot to see in the world of golf. Enjoy and learn about this great sport for years to come!

"Develop a passion for learning. If you do, you will never cease to grow better."

- Anthony (Tony) J. D'Angelo

Conclusion

You will save strokes doing the 54 easy things in this book. Keep this book in your bag to help remind you it's not hard to save strokes. Your golf will become more enjoyable.

St. Andrews

Thank you for reading this book. We hope you found it entertaining and had a few laughs too.

If you enjoyed reading it, please consider leaving a review on Amazon so more readers can find this title.

We love questions or comments; so, don't be shy and feel free to contact us.

Thank you again.

Team Golfwell

info@teamgolfwell.com

www.TeamGolfwell.com

Team Golfwell's Other Books

<u>Absolutely Hilarious Adult Golf Joke Book</u>

Team Golfwell's Other Books

Fascinating Golf Stories and More Hilarious Adult Golf Jokes

(Second in the Golfwell Adult Joke Book Series)

Team Golfwell's Other Books

Great Golf Formats: Betting Games, Adult Golf Jokes and Stories

(Third in the Golfwell Adult Joke Book Series)

Team Golfwell's Other Books

TEAM GOLFWELL

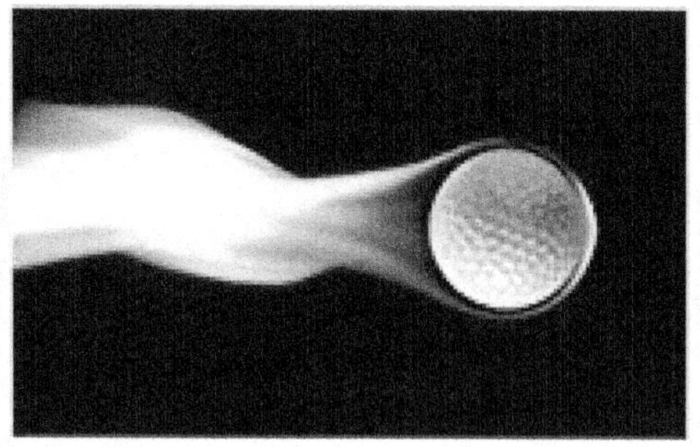

GOLF TIPS

AND ADULT GOLF JOKES

Golf Tips and Adult Golf Jokes

(Fourth in Golfwell Adult Joke Book Series)

Team Golfwell's Other Books

Golf Shots: How To Easily Learn a Wide Variety of Shots

Team Golfwell's Other Books

Golf Driving Techniques from Golfing Greats and Golf Stories

Team Golfwell's Other Books

Golf Putting Techniques from Golfing Greats: Proven Putting Techniques from Tiger, Rory, Jason Day, Jordan Spieth, and Others

Team Golfwell's Other Books

WALK THE WINNING WAYS OF GOLF'S GREATESTS

GOLFING GREATS' ADVICE TO YOUNG GOLFERS

Walk the Winning Ways of Golf's Greatests

Team at Golfwell's Other Books

Golf FitnessGolf Fitness: An All-Inclusive Golf Fitness Program For Golfers Only

More about the Team Golfwell

Printed in Great Britain
by Amazon